LE CORDON BLEU

HOME COLLECTION

PUDDINGS & COBBLERS

PERIPLUS

contents

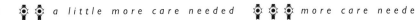

recipe ratings ✷ *easy* ✷✷ *a little more care needed* ✷✷✷ *more care needed*

Chocolate and cardamom brioche pudding

A delicious variation on an old favorite, this bread pudding is made with rich, yeasty brioche and dark chocolate, and is flavored with cardamom pods to give an aromatic twist.

Preparation time **45 minutes + 40 minutes resting**
Total cooking time **50 minutes**
Serves 4–6

1³/4 cups milk
I vanilla bean, split lengthwise
5 cardamom pods, lightly crushed
5 oz. brioche loaf, cut into ¹/2 inch slices
2 tablespoons unsalted butter, softened
3 eggs
3 tablespoons sugar
**3¹/4 oz. good-quality bittersweet or semisweet
   chocolate, finely chopped**
confectioner's sugar, for dusting

1 Slowly bring the milk, vanilla bean and cardamom pods to a boil in a saucepan. Remove from the stove, then set aside for about 30 minutes for the flavors to infuse. Preheat the oven to 315°F and brush a 9-inch oval pie plate or ovenproof dish with a little melted butter.
2 Spread one side of each brioche slice with the softened butter. Cut each slice into four triangles and remove the crusts. Neatly overlap them in the prepared dish, standing the triangles up a little.

3 Whisk the eggs and sugar in a heatproof bowl until pale and thick. Bring the milk back to a boil, then remove from the heat, add the chocolate and stir until the chocolate has melted and the mixture is smooth. Add the chocolate mixture to the egg and sugar mixture and stir well, then strain into a bowl and discard the cardamom pods and vanilla bean.
4 Pour three-fourths of the chocolate liquid onto the brioche until each slice is soaked in the liquid, then rest for 10 minutes for the liquid to soak in. Pour over the remaining chocolate liquid. If you want a crunchier topping, sprinkle the surface of the pudding with a little extra sugar.
5 Place the dish inside a baking pan and pour in enough hot water to come halfway up its sides. Bake for 40–45 minutes, or until the custard is set.
6 Remove the pudding from the oven and if you didn't sprinkle the surface with sugar, dust with a small amount of sifted confectioner's sugar. Serve with a spoonful of crème fraîche.

Chef's tip For a variation, omit the cardamom pods and instead spread a handful of well-drained, canned black cherries evenly over the base of the dish or between the brioche slices.

Traditional Christmas pudding

Also known as plum pudding, Christmas pudding is a very dense steamed pudding that tastes a bit like spice cake. It can be made up to a year in advance and reheated in just a few hours on Christmas day.

Preparation time **45 minutes + overnight marinating**
Total cooking time **10 hours**
Serves **8**

MARINATED FRUITS
2 cups golden raisins
2 cups raisins
2 cups dried currants
1/4 cup candied cherries
1/4 cup candied citrus peel
1/3 cup pitted and chopped dates
1 1/2 teaspoons pumpkin pie spice
1 teaspoon ground cinnamon
1 teaspoon ground nutmeg
1/4 teaspoon ground ginger
grated zest of 2 oranges
juice of 1 orange
grated zest of 1 lemon
1/2 cup beer
1/2 cup brandy

PUDDING
1 2/3 cups peeled, cored and grated apples
1 1/4 cups all-purpose flour
1/2 cup ground almonds or almond meal
6 1/2 oz. suet, grated (see page 63)
3/4 cup dark brown sugar
2 1/2 cups fresh white bread crumbs

2 eggs, beaten
2 tablespoons molasses

3 tablespoons brandy

1 To prepare the marinated fruits, put all ingredients into a large bowl and mix together well. Cover with plastic wrap and leave overnight in a cool place.

2 The next day, prepare the pudding by putting all the ingredients into a large bowl and making a well in the center. Add the marinated fruits and any liquid and mix well to form a soft batter.

3 Prepare one 10-cup or two 5-cup pudding basins or heatproof glass bowls for steaming (see Chef's techniques, page 62). Steam the pudding for 10 hours, following the steaming method in the Chef's techniques on page 62.

4 Allow the pudding to stand for 15 minutes before removing the string, aluminum foil and paper and unmolding. In a saucepan, warm the brandy, then at the table pour it over the pudding and ignite it at arm's length. Serve with traditional brandy hard sauce or cream.

Chef's tip To prepare this pudding ahead of time, steam for 8 hours, then leave to cool. Remove the string, foil and paper and check that the surface of the pudding is dry. Re-cover with new paper and foil and store in the refrigerator until needed. To reheat for serving, steam for 2 hours, then leave for 15 minutes and serve as above.

Fruit cobbler

The name "cobbler" originates from the nineteenth century and refers to a fruit pie with a scone topping. This cobbler has a golden hazelnut and apricot topping over summer's late fruit.

*Preparation time **1 hour + 20 minutes refrigeration***
*Total cooking time **40 minutes***
Serves 6

TOPPING

2¼ cups all-purpose flour
2 teaspoons baking powder
5 tablespoons unsalted butter, chilled and cut in cubes
3 tablespoons sugar
2 eggs, beaten
3 tablespoons milk
¾ cup finely chopped hazelnuts (filberts)
2½ oz. dried apricots, finely chopped

COMPOTE

¼ cup sugar
1½ tablespoons unsalted butter
2 cloves
1 cinnamon stick
½ vanilla bean, split lengthwise
2 Granny Smith apples, peeled, cored and cut in eighths
2 ripe pears, peeled, cored and cut into
**   ¾ inch pieces**
3 fresh apricots, halved and pitted,
**   or 6 canned apricot halves**
2 fresh peaches, halved, pitted and cut in eight pieces,
**   or 4 canned peach halves, sliced**
3 fresh plums, halved and pitted, or
**   3 canned and pitted dark plums, halved**
finely grated zest of 1 lemon
finely grated zest of ½ orange
pinch of ground pumpkin pie spice
pinch of ground cinnamon

1 egg yolk
confectioner's sugar, for dusting

1 Brush a round 8½ x 1½ inch ovenproof dish with melted butter.

2 To make the topping, sift the flour and baking powder into a bowl. Rub the butter into the flour using your fingertips until the mixture resembles fine bread crumbs. Lightly stir in the sugar, make a well in the center and add the eggs and milk. Bring the mixture roughly together using a pastry blender. Add the hazelnuts and apricots and stir the ingredients together to form a dough, then shape into a ball and flatten slightly. Wrap in plastic wrap and place in the refrigerator for about 20 minutes.

3 To make the compote, first prepare a caramel using the sugar and 3 tablespoons water, following the method in the Chef's techniques on page 62. After the caramel has stopped cooking, return to the heat and remelt the caramel gently, then mix in the butter, cloves, cinnamon stick, vanilla bean and apples and cook, covered, for 5 minutes. Add the pears, apricots, peaches and fresh plums, cover and gently cook for about 5 minutes, stirring occasionally. (If using canned plums, add at the end of the 5 minutes cooking time or they will break up.) Discard the flavorings, stir in the lemon and orange zest and the ground spices, and pour the compote into the prepared dish.

4 Preheat the oven to 415°F. On a lightly floured surface, roll out the topping dough to ⅝ inch thick, then cut out circles using a 2½-inch plain cutter. Arrange the circles, slightly overlapping, on top of the hot compote.

5 Beat the egg yolk and 1 teaspoon water together to make an egg wash and brush over the top of the cobbler. Do not brush the cut sides or the egg will set and prevent rising. Bake for 15 minutes, or until well risen and golden brown. Cool for 5–10 minutes before serving, then dust with sifted confectioner's sugar and serve with cream or ice cream.

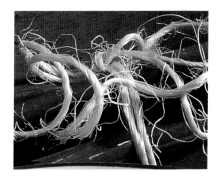

Rhubarb crumble

Also called a rhubarb crisp, this simple dessert is a great way to use up excess ripe, in-season fruit.
In this version, tangy rhubarb perfectly complements the buttery, crumbly topping.

*Preparation time **30 minutes***
*Total cooking time **40 minutes***
Serves 6

2 tablespoons strawberry jam
5 cups trimmed rhubarb, cut in 1 inch slices
2 tablespoons Demerara or turbinado sugar
1/3 cup whole wheat flour
1/2 cup all-purpose flour
6 tablespoons unsalted butter, chilled and cut
  into cubes
1/2 cup granulated, Demerara or turbinado sugar
1 tablespoon pumpkin seeds, toasted
1 tablespoon hazelnuts (filberts), toasted and
  roughly chopped

1 Put the strawberry jam in a wide, shallow frying pan with 2 tablespoons water, then add the rhubarb in a single layer with the 2 tablespoons of Demerara or turbinado sugar. Bring to a boil, then immediately lower the heat to a simmer, cover tightly with a lid or piece of aluminum foil and cook for about 5 minutes. The acidity of rhubarb does vary quite a lot, so taste and add more sugar if necessary.

2 Transfer the rhubarb into a 5-cup, 8 x 2 1/2 inch ovenproof dish. Spread out evenly, then pour over enough rhubarb juice to come halfway up the rhubarb. Set aside to cool. Preheat the oven to 350°F.

3 Sift the whole wheat and all-purpose flours into a larfe bowl, tipping the bits left in the seive from the whole wheat flour back into the bowl. Rub the butter into the flour using your fingertips until the mixture resembles fine bread crumbs. Continue to rub in the butter until small lumps begin to form, then add the sugar, pumpkin seeds and the chopped hazelnuts and toss to incorporate.

4 Scatter the crumble mixture evenly over the rhubarb in the dish without pressing it down, then bake for 20–30 minutes, or until the topping is golden brown. Dust with a little extra sugar if you wish, and serve warm or cold with whipped cream.

Eve's pudding

As the name of this English dessert suggests, it should be made with apples, which take on a tempting caramelized sweetness under the light sponge cake and golden almonds.

Preparation time 25 minutes
Total cooking time 45 minutes
Serves 6

COMPOTE
3¹/₂ tablespoons unsalted butter, softened
¹/₃ cup sugar
2 cloves
¹/₂ teaspoon ground cinnamon
I vanilla bean, split lengthwise
4–5, about I¹/₂ lb. Golden Delicious apples, peeled,
    cored and cut into eight pieces

ALMOND TOPPING
¹/₂ cup unsalted butter, at room temperature
¹/₂ cup sugar
finely grated zest of I lemon
¹/₂ teaspoon vanilla extract
3 eggs, beaten
¹/₄ cup all-purpose flour
²/₃ cup ground almonds or almond meal, sifted
³/₄ cup sliced almonds

2 tablespoons apricot jam
confectioner's sugar, for dusting

1 Brush a 6-cup ovenproof baking dish, 3/4 inch deep, with melted butter.

2 To make the compote, put the butter and sugar in a saucepan and stir over low heat to melt the butter and dissolve the sugar. Add the cloves, cinnamon and vanilla bean, then add the apples and mix to coat with the butter mixture. Cover and cook very gently for 5 minutes, or until the apples are just starting to soften. Discard the flavorings and spread evenly over the base of the prepared dish. Leave to cool. Preheat the oven to 350°F.

3 To make the topping, put the butter, sugar, lemon zest and vanilla in a bowl and, using a wooden spoon or electric mixer, beat until light and creamy. Add the beaten eggs in six additions, beating well between each addition. Sift the flour and a pinch of salt onto the mixture, scatter on the ground almonds and, using a large metal spoon or spatula, fold in gently to combine. Spoon over the apple mixture, smooth the top and sprinkle with the sliced almonds. Bake for 30–35 minutes, or until the topping is firm to the touch.

4 In a small saucepan, heat the apricot jam with 2 teaspoons water. When the mixture has melted and begins to boil, strain it into a small bowl and, while still hot, brush it over the surface of the dessert. Leave for 1 minute, then dust with sifted confectioner's sugar. Serve with whipped cream.

Ginger pudding with kumquat and ginger compote

*This warming winter steamed pudding is made with molasses and ginger and is
a perfect match for the tart kumquat and ginger compote.*

Preparation time 1 hour 30 minutes + overnight resting
Total cooking time 2 hours 30 minutes
Serves 6

COMPOTE
1 1/2 lbs. ripe kumquats, quartered and seeded
2 cups sugar
1/3 cup preserved stem ginger, chopped
    (drained weight, reserving 1/2 cup syrup)

GINGER PUDDING
2/3 cup preserved stem ginger (drained weight,
    reserving 1 tablespoon syrup)
1 tablespoon golden syrup or dark corn syrup
1/2 cup unsalted butter, at room temperature
1/2 cup light brown sugar
1 tablespoon molasses
3 eggs, beaten
1 1/2 cups self-rising flour
1 teaspoon ground ginger
2 tablespoons milk

1 To make the compote, put the kumquats, sugar and ginger in a bowl and stir to combine. Cover and let stand overnight in a cool place to allow the sugar to dissolve and the juice to start running from the fruit.
2 Tip the fruit and sugary juices into a large saucepan and add the ginger syrup and 2 cups water. Slowly bring to a boil over low heat, stirring until any remaining sugar has dissolved. Skim off any surface foam with a metal spoon. Raise the heat and boil hard, without stirring, for 15–20 minutes, or until the compote has thickened and is slightly syrupy. Remove from heat and allow to cool.

3 To make the pudding, prepare a 5-cup pudding basin or heatproof glass bowl for steaming (see Chef's techniques, page 62).
4 Slice just over half the ginger thinly, then finely dice the remainder. Using the ginger slices, arrange a five-petal flower in the bottom of the basin or bowl, then continue to form flower patterns up the sides of the basin or bowl until they reach two-thirds of the way up.
5 In a small saucepan, gently warm the syrup so it flows easily, then pour it into the bottom of the basin or bowl without dislodging the ginger flowers.
6 Put the butter and sugar in a bowl and, using a wooden spoon or electric mixer, beat together until light and creamy, then stir in the molasses and reserved ginger syrup. Add the beaten eggs in six additions, beating well between each addition. Sift the flour, ground ginger and a pinch of salt onto the mixture and fold in using a large metal spoon or plastic spatula, then briskly fold in the milk and diced ginger.
7 Spoon the mixture into the prepared basin or bowl, cover and steam for 2 hours, following the steaming method in the Chef's techniques on page 62. To test when the pudding is done, pierce with a skewer. If it comes out clean, the pudding is cooked. Remove the string, foil and paper and unmold. Serve with the compote and some lightly whipped cream.

Chef's tips To store excess compote, sterilize some jars and lids by washing them in hot soapy water. Rinse, then dry in an oven at 250°F for 20 minutes. Pour in the compote, seal the jars, date and store somewhere cool. Use as a sauce for ice cream.

Look for golden syrup in stores that specialize in European imports.

Schmarrn

Kaiserschmarrn is a deliciously simple Austrian dessert of fried crêpes, often served with a fruit compote. This variation includes the crêpes, a fruity plum marmalade and smooth custard all in one dish.

*Preparation time **1 hour + 30 minutes refrigeration + 15 minutes cooling***
*Total cooking time **1 hour 45 minutes***
Serves 6

CREPES
1/2 cup all-purpose flour
1 tablespoon sugar
1 egg
1/4 teaspoon vanilla extract
3/4 cup milk
clarified butter or oil, for frying

MARMALADE
3/4 lb. fresh red plums, pitted and roughly chopped
    or 1 3/4 lb. canned plums, drained, pitted and
    roughly chopped
1/3 cup sugar
1 cinnamon stick
1/2 vanilla bean, split lengthwise

CUSTARD
3/4 cup milk
3/4 cup cream
1 vanilla bean, split lengthwise
3 eggs
1 egg yolk
1/3 cup sugar

3 tablespoons apricot jam
1/3 cup toasted sliced almonds
confectioner's sugar, for dusting

1 To make the crêpes, sift the flour into a bowl with the sugar and a small pinch of salt. Make a well in the center, add the egg and vanilla and begin to whisk in the flour. As it starts to thicken, add the milk gradually until all the flour is incorporated and the batter is smooth. Cover and refrigerate for 30 minutes.

2 Cook the crêpes following the method in the Chef's techniques on page 63, turning out finished ones onto a sheet of waxed paper and covering with a dish towel.

3 To make the marmalade, put the plums, sugar (the plums will need less sugar if they are very ripe), cinnamon stick and vanilla bean in a saucepan and cook, covered, over low heat for 15 minutes, or until the mixture is soft and very thick. If there is too much juice, remove the lid and cook, uncovered, until the plums have a sticky, jam-like consistency. Set aside to cool for 15 minutes, then remove the cinnamon and vanilla bean.

4 Spread the plum marmalade over the crêpes and roll up tightly to form long cigar shapes. Slice into 1/2 inch pieces. Brush a shallow 4-cup ovenproof dish with butter, then arrange the crêpes in it, cut-side-up. Preheat the oven to 350°F.

5 To make the custard, put the milk, cream and vanilla bean in a saucepan and bring slowly to a boil. Remove from the heat. In a bowl, using a wooden spoon or electric mixer, cream together the eggs, yolk and sugar until pale and thick. Pour the hot milk onto the eggs and mix well, then discard the bean and strain into a bowl.

6 Pour the custard over the crêpes and place the dish inside a baking dish. Pour in enough hot water to come halfway up its sides. Bake for 40 minutes, or until the top is firm to the touch.

7 In a small saucepan, heat the apricot jam with 1 tablespoon water. When the mixture has melted and begins to boil, strain it into a small bowl and, while still hot, brush it over the surface of the dessert. Leave to cool, then decorate with the almonds and sifted confectioner's sugar. Serve with cream.

Queen of puddings

*A classic English dessert that dates back to the nineteenth century, the Queen of puddings is created
from layers of smooth custard, soft red fruit and jam, all topped with a crisp crown of meringue.*

Preparation time **25 minutes**
Total cooking time **35 minutes**
Serves 6

FRUIT PUREE
3 cups raspberries or strawberries
lemon juice, to taste
confectioner's sugar, to taste

5 tablespoons unsalted butter
2 cups fresh bread or cake crumbs
2/3 cup sugar
finely grated zest of 1 lemon
6 egg yolks
3/4 cup fresh raspberries
3/4 cup fresh strawberries, quartered
3/4 cup fresh blueberries
1/3 cup raspberry jam
4 egg whites
confectioner's sugar, for dusting

1 Preheat the oven to 350°F. Brush a 10 x 7 inch
shallow ovenproof dish with melted butter.
2 To make the fruit purée, put the raspberries or
strawberries in a blender or food processor and process.

Add lemon juice and confectioner's sugar to taste,
depending on the ripeness of the fruit, then pass the
purée through a fine sieve.
3 In a saucepan, melt the butter, then remove from the
heat. Place the bread or cake crumbs, 2 tablespoons of
the sugar and the lemon zest in a bowl and combine.
Make a well in the center and pour in the fruit purée,
melted butter and the egg yolks and beat to form a
smooth paste.
4 Arrange the raspberries, strawberries and blueberries
in the prepared dish and pour the egg mixture over
the fruit. Bake for 25 minutes, or until set. Remove from
the oven and allow to cool a little. Raise the oven
temperature to 400°F.
5 Soften the raspberry jam by beating it in a small bowl
with a wooden spoon, then gently spread over the
cooked fruit and custard base in the dish.
6 Place the egg whites in a clean dry bowl and beat
with a hand whisk or electric mixer until soft peaks
form. Gradually add the remaining sugar, beating well
between each addition, until stiff glossy peaks form.
Spoon into a pastry bag with a large star tip.
7 Pipe the meringue around the edge of the dish. Dust
with sifted confectioner's sugar and bake for 3–5 minutes,
or until the meringue is golden brown and crisp. Serve
warm or cold with cream.

Lemon and lavender rice soufflés

These light soufflé puddings combine the freshness of lemon with the gentle aroma of lavender.

Preparation time **15 minutes + cooling**
Total cooking time **1 hour 15 minutes**
Serves 6–8

1/3 cup long-grain rice
3 cups milk
finely grated zest of 1 lemon
1/2 teaspoon dried lavender, finely chopped
1/2 vanilla bean, split lengthwise
1 egg white
3 tablespoons sugar

1 Put the rice in a strainer and rinse thoroughly under running water until the water runs clear, then drain.

2 Pour the milk into a heavy-bottomed saucepan, add the lemon zest, lavender, vanilla bean and rice and slowly bring to a boil. Reduce the heat and simmer, stirring often, for 40 minutes, or until the mixture is soft and creamy and when a spoon drawn across the base of the saucepan, leaves a soft parting line behind. Set aside to cool completely.

3 Preheat the oven to 350°F. Lightly brush eight 3 x 1 1/2 inch ramekins or an oval 9 1/2 x 1 1/2 inch ovenproof dish with melted butter.

4 Put the egg white in a clean dry bowl and beat with a hand whisk or electric beaters until soft peaks form. Add half the sugar and beat until stiff glossy peaks form. Sprinkle on the remaining sugar and, using a plastic spatula or a large metal spoon, gently fold in to form meringue. Check that the rice is still creamy (add a tablespoon of cold milk if necessary), then remove the vanilla bean and fold in the meringue.

5 Fill the prepared dishes three-quarters full, place on a baking sheet and bake for 20–25 minutes, or until well risen and golden brown. Serve with berries and cream.

Spotted dick

The origin of the name of this classic English suet and raisin steamed pudding is not known, though it seems that dick may have been a general nineteenth-century term for pudding. Spotted dick is sometimes known by the equally unusual name of Spotted dog.

Preparation time 15 minutes + 1 hour soaking
Total cooking time 2 hours
Serves 6–8

2/3 cup currants
1 cup raisins
2 tablespoons brandy
2 cups self-rising flour
1/2 cup grated suet (see page 63)
grated zest of 1 lemon
pinch of grated nutmeg
3 tablespoons sugar
1/2 cup milk

1 Put the currants, raisins and brandy in a bowl, cover with plastic wrap and set aside for at least 1 hour, or overnight, to soak.

2 Sift the flour and a pinch of salt into a bowl and stir in the suet, lemon zest, nutmeg and sugar. Add the soaked fruit and brandy, then the milk, and mix with a wooden spoon to form a firm dough.

3 Lay a sheet of waxed paper on a work surface and form the mixture into a roll shape, 8 inches long. Roll the pudding in the paper and fold up the ends, taking care not to wrap it too tightly as the pudding will expand as it cooks.

4 Wrap the roll in a dish towel, put in the top of a bamboo or metal steamer, cover and steam for 2 hours. Do not let the pudding boil dry—replenish with boiling water as it cooks. Unroll from the paper, cut into slices and serve with custard sauce or cream.

Chef's tip If your steamer will not accommodate an 8-inch pudding, make the pudding shorter and fatter and cook for 15–20 minutes longer.

Rum babas

These spongy cakes soaked in a rum syrup are said to have been named by a Polish king after his storybook hero, Ali Baba. Here they are served with a vanilla-flavored Chantilly cream and fresh fruit.

Preparation time 1 hour + 1 hour rising
Total cooking time 30 minutes
Serves 8

DOUGH
2 cups all-purpose or bread flour
1 teaspoon salt
1 teaspoon sugar
1/2 oz. fresh yeast or 1/4 oz. dry yeast
1/3 cup milk
3 eggs, beaten
1/2 cup raisins, soaked in 1 tablespoon rum
3 tablespoons melted butter, just warm

SYRUP
2 cups water
3/4 cup sugar
zest of 1 lemon
1 cardamom pod
2 bay leaves
1/2 orange, roughly chopped
2 tablespoons dark rum

CHANTILLY CREAM
1 1/4 cups heavy cream
1 tablespoon confectioner's sugar
1/2 teaspoon vanilla extract

3 tablespoons apricot jam
fresh fruit, such as strawberries and raspberries,
   to decorate

1 Brush eight individual pudding molds or a 4-cup ring mold with melted butter, then dust with some flour and tap out the excess.

2 To make the dough, sift the flour, salt and sugar into a large bowl and make a well in the center. Put the yeast in a small bowl. In a small saucepan, warm the milk until tepid, then add to the yeast. Stir to dissolve, then mix in 1 tablespoon flour and set aside until foamy. When foamy, add to the beaten eggs and pour into the well in the flour. Prepare the dough following the method in the Chef's techniques on page 63. Preheat the oven to 415°F.

3 Bake the babas for 12 minutes (25 minutes for a large one), or until golden. Loosen the babas and turn out of the molds onto a wire rack to cool. Prick all over with a fine skewer.

4 To make the syrup, gently heat all the ingredients except the rum together in a medium saucepan, stirring to dissolve the sugar, then bring to a boil and boil for about 15 minutes to reduce the syrup and thicken slightly. Remove the pan from the stove and leave for 5 minutes to infuse the flavors. Strain, discard the flavorings, return the syrup to the pan and reheat. Remove from the stove and stir in the rum. Pour the syrup into a shallow dish and roll the cold babas in the hot syrup. Place the babas on a wire rack over a plate to drip off excess syrup and to cool completely.

5 To make the Chantilly cream, pour the cream into a bowl and add the confectioner's sugar and vanilla. Using a hand whisk or electric mixer, whip the cream until it just forms soft peaks that hold as the whisk is lifted from the bowl.

6 In a small pan, heat the apricot jam with 1 tablespoon water. When the mixture has melted and begins to boil, strain it into a small bowl and, while still hot, brush it over the babas, then leave to cool.

7 Serve the babas with the Chantilly cream and fruit. If you have made a large rum baba, fill the centre of the ring with the cream and fruit.

Layered black currant pudding

This sharp but fruity steamed pudding can be made with fresh or frozen berries. Use red currants or blueberries if you can't find black currants.

Preparation time **35 minutes**
Total cooking time **2 hours**
Serves 6

3/4 cup unsalted butter, at room temperature
3/4 cup sugar
grated zest of 1 lemon
3 eggs, beaten
1 1/3 cups self-rising flour
3 tablespoons milk
4 tablespoons black currant jam, beaten until smooth
1/3 cup frozen black currants, thawed, or fresh black currants, stalks and ends removed

1 Prepare a 5-cup pudding basin or heatproof glass bowl for steaming (see Chef's techniques, page 62).

2 Put the butter and sugar in a bowl and, using a wooden spoon or electric mixer, beat together until light and creamy. Add the zest, then the beaten eggs in six additions, beating well between each addition. Sift the flour and a pinch of salt onto the mixture and fold in using a large metal spoon or plastic spatula, then quickly fold in the milk.

3 Place a tablespoon of jam in the base of the prepared basin or bowl and arrange the black currants on top. Spread a quarter of the sponge mixture over the fruit, followed by a tablespoon of the jam. Continue layering, with the last layer being the remaining sponge mixture. Cover and steam for 2 hours, following the steaming method in the Chef's techniques on page 62. To test when the pudding is done, pierce with a skewer. If it comes out clean, the pudding is cooked.

4 Allow the pudding to stand for 15 minutes before removing the string, foil and paper and turning out. Serve with crème anglaise (see page 43).

Crunchy pear pudding

*This dessert, with its perfect combination of warm cinnamon-pear filling and crunchy hazelnut topping,
is a great way to use ripe pears when they're in season.*

Preparation time **30 minutes**
Total cooking time **1 hour 45 minutes**
Serves **4–6**

FILLING
4 tablespoons unsalted butter
1/2 cup Demerara or turbinado sugar
finely grated zest of 1 orange
finely grated zest of 1 lemon
1/2 teaspoon cinnamon
**6 ripe pears (about 2 lb. in total), peeled, cored
   and cut into 1/2 inch cubes**

TOPPING
5 tablespoons unsalted butter
4 tablespoons sugar
2 tablespoons golden syrup or dark corn syrup
1 1/2 cups rolled oats
**3/4 cup hazelnuts (filberts), skins removed, roasted
   and roughly crushed**
1 cup self-rising flour
1 egg, beaten

1 tablespoon sugar
1/2 teaspoon ground cinnamon

1   To make the filling, put the butter, sugar, orange and lemon zest and the cinnamon in a saucepan and heat gently for about 5 minutes, stirring to dissolve the sugar. Increase the heat to medium and cook for another 5 minutes, or until the mixture bubbles and looks golden. Add the pears and cook gently for 8–10 minutes, or until the pieces are just tender. Remove from the stove and leave the pears to cool in the pan.

2   To make the topping, put the butter, sugar, syrup and 2 teaspoons water in a saucepan and heat gently, stirring until smooth. Bring to a boil, then remove from the stove and stir in the oats, hazelnuts, flour and egg.

3   Spoon a third of the topping into the bottom of a 6 1/2 x 2 1/2 inch heatproof round dish. Use the back of a spoon to flatten and press the mixture against the bottom and a little way up the sides, to a thickness of 1/2 inch. Using a slotted spoon, remove the pears from the pan and place in the dish, then add 4 tablespoons of juice from the pan. Spoon the remaining topping over the pears and spread evenly to cover, then lightly smooth the top using the back of the spoon. Cover with foil and seal well around the edge of the dish by tying a piece of string around the foil.

4   Place a saucer or trivet in a large saucepan and set the dish on it. Pour in boiling water to come halfway up the dish and bring to a boil on top of the stove. Cover and steam the pudding for 1 hour 20 minutes, or until the topping feels firm when pressed, adding more boiling water if needed.

5   Remove the dish from the water and wipe it dry. Mix together the sugar and the cinnamon and dust over the top. Serve with ice cream or crème anglaise (see page 43).

Chef's tip Look for golden syrup in stores that specialize in European imports.

Chocolate chip pudding with chocolate sauce

This recipe provides a double-chocolate hit, with a rich hot or cold chocolate sauce to pour over a chocolate chip pudding. Alternatively, you could serve the dessert with just cream or crème anglaise.

*Preparation time **45 minutes***
*Total cooking time **2 hours 15 minutes***
Serves 6

1/2 cup unsalted butter, at room temperature
2/3 cup light brown sugar
1 teaspoon vanilla extract
4 eggs, beaten
1 cup self-rising flour
1/4 cup unsweetened cocoa powder
1 tablespoon milk
1 oz. dark chocolate chips
1 3/4 oz. white chocolate chips

CHOCOLATE SAUCE
1 cup sugar
3 1/4 oz. good-quality dark chocolate, chopped
2 tablespoons unsweetened cocoa powder, sifted

1 Prepare a 5-cup pudding basin or heatproof glass bowl for steaming (see Chef's techniques, page 62).
2 Put the butter and sugar in a bowl and, using a wooden spoon or electric mixer, beat together until light and creamy, then mix in the vanilla. Add the eggs in six additions, beating well between each addition. Sift the flour, cocoa powder and a pinch of salt onto the mixture and fold in using a large metal spoon or plastic spatula, then quickly fold in the milk and both the dark and white chocolate chips.
3 Spoon the mixture into the prepared basin or bowl, cover and steam for 2 hours, following the steaming method in the Chef's techniques on page 62. To test when the pudding is done, pierce with a skewer. If it comes out clean, the pudding is cooked.
4 To make the sauce, put 1 1/4 cups water in a saucepan with the sugar and chocolate. Bring to a boil slowly, stirring continuously to dissolve the sugar, then remove from the heat. Mix the cocoa with 4 teaspoons water to form a smooth paste, add to the pan, stir and return to medium heat. Bring back to a boil, whisking vigorously, then simmer for 5 minutes without allowing the sauce to boil. Strain through a fine strainer and leave to cool a little. The chocolate sauce can be served warm or cold.
5 Remove the string, foil and paper from the pudding and allow to stand for 5–10 minutes before turning out. Serve with the chocolate sauce.

Chef's tip For a more chocolate-flavored pudding, replace the white chocolate chips with dark chips.

Maple pudding

*This family favorite, a steamed pudding, is served with a delicious cinnamon-flavored syrup
that should be poured over just before serving.*

Preparation time **35 minutes**
Total cooking time **2 hours**
Serves 6

I cup unsalted butter, at room temperature
I cup sugar
4 eggs, beaten
1/2 teaspoon vanilla extract
finely grated zest of 2 lemons
2 cups self-rising flour
1/3 cup maple syrup

SAUCE
I cinnamon stick
1/4 vanilla bean
1/2 cup maple syrup
grated zest and juice of I lemon

1 Prepare an 8-cup pudding basin or heatproof glass bowl for steaming (see Chef's techniques, page 62).

2 Put the butter and sugar in a bowl and, using a wooden spoon or electric mixer, beat together until light and creamy. Add the eggs in six additions, beating well between each addition, then mix in the vanilla and lemon zest. Sift the flour onto the mixture and fold in using a large metal spoon or plastic spatula.

3 Place the syrup in the bottom of the basin or bowl and spoon the sponge mixture on top. Cover and steam for 1 hour 40 minutes, following the steaming method in the Chef's techniques on page 62. To test when the pudding is done, pierce with a skewer. If it comes out clean, the pudding is cooked (though it may still look a bit sticky from the syrup).

4 To make the sauce, put the cinnamon, vanilla, syrup, lemon juice and zest and 1 1/4 cups water in a saucepan and bring to a boil. Simmer for about 15 minutes to reduce by one-third, then remove and discard the cinnamon stick and vanilla bean.

5 Allow the pudding to stand for 10 minutes before removing the string, foil and paper. Serve with the maple syrup sauce.

Sticky toffee puddings

Dates are the secret ingredient that makes these little desserts so wickedly delicious,
while the toffee sauce ensures they remain famously sticky.

Preparation time **40 minutes + 1 hour soaking**
Total cooking time **40 minutes**
Serves 10

I cup pitted and chopped dates
1/3 cup raisins
grated zest of 1/2 lemon
I teaspoon baking soda
2 tablespoons coffee extract or I tablespoon instant
  coffee mixed with 2 tablespoons boiling water
3 1/2 tablespoons unsalted butter, at room temperature
I cup light brown sugar
4 eggs, beaten
2 cups self-rising flour

SAUCE
I vanilla bean, split lengthwise
4 tablespoons unsalted butter
2/3 cup Demerara or turbinado sugar
1/2 cup heavy cream

1 Brush ten 2/3-cup pudding molds or ramekins with melted butter and chill before brushing with butter again, then dust with flour and tap out the excess. Preheat the oven to 350°F.

2 Put the dates, raisins and lemon zest in a bowl. Sprinkle with the baking soda and coffee extract, pour on 1 cup boiling water, cover and set aside to soak for one hour.

3 Put the butter and sugar in a bowl and, using a wooden spoon or electric mixer, beat until light and creamy. Add the eggs in six additions, beating well between each addition. Sift the flour and a pinch of salt onto the mixture and fold in using a large metal spoon or plastic spatula. Add the date and raisin mixture with its liquid and stir gently to make a loose batter.

4 Spoon the mixture into the molds to three-quarters full. Make a slight hollow in the center of the mixture and bake for about 20–30 minutes, or until springy to the touch.

5 To make the sauce, scrape the vanilla seeds into a saucepan and add the bean, butter, sugar and cream and stir for about 3 minutes to dissolve the sugar, then simmer over medium-low heat, without stirring, until smooth and golden brown. Remove and discard the vanilla bean, set the sauce aside and keep warm.

6 When the puddings are cooked, allow to stand for 10 minutes, then turn out. Serve warm with the toffee sauce and whipped cream.

Chef's tip If 10 puddings are too many, you could either halve the recipe or freeze the extra puddings. When you are ready to use the frozen puddings, defrost, then wrap in aluminum foil and reheat in a 350°F oven for about 20 minutes.

Summer puddings

Perfect for entertaining, these pretty English puddings need to be prepared the day before to allow the fruit juices to flavor the bread and turn it that distinctive vivid pink color.

Preparation time **30 minutes + overnight refrigeration**
Total cooking time **5 minutes**
Serves 6

18 thin slices good-quality 1-day-old white bread
2 lb. mixed soft fruits, such as blackberries,
  raspberries, strawberries and black currants,
  fresh or frozen and hulled
up to 1/2 cup sugar, depending on the sweetness
  of the fruit

1 Cut the crusts from the bread and discard. Reserving two or three slices for the top, cut circles and strips out of the remaining slices to fit the base and sides of six 1/2-cup ramekins or pudding molds, or a 4-cup pudding basin or heatproof glass bowl. Make sure the base and sides are completely lined and that there are no spaces between the slices of bread.

2 Halve or quarter the strawberries if large, then put all the fruit in a large saucepan with 2 tablespoons water and add the sugar, to taste. Cover and cook over low heat for about 5 minutes, or until the juices are running from the fruit and they are just tender but still whole.

3 Ladle the fruit and juices into the bread-lined ramekins, molds, basin or bowl until it reaches almost to the top of the bread, reserving any excess. Cover with the reserved slices of bread, trimming to fit snugly onto the surface of the fruit. Place on a baking sheet to catch any excess juices and cover with a plate and a weight of about 2 lb. if using the basin or bowl, or smaller weights if using the ramekins or molds (you can use cans). Chill overnight in the refrigerator.

4 When ready to serve, remove the weights and carefully unmold the puddings. Serve cold with the extra fruit and juice spooned over and a sorbet, ice cream or cream.

Chef's tip For the best color and texture, use fewer strawberries than the other softer and darker fruit.

Pineapple and coconut upside-down cake

A delicious variation on the traditional pineapple recipe. The caramelized topping that characterizes an upside-down cake is created during baking by the combination of sugar, butter and fruit juices.

Preparation time **30 minutes**
Total cooking time **1 hour 5 minutes**
Serves 6

1/2 cup sugar
3 1/2 tablespoons unsalted butter
5–7 canned pineapple slices, well drained
7 candied cherries, halved

COCONUT SPONGE CAKE
2/3 cup unsalted butter, at room temperature
2/3 cup sugar
4 eggs
finely grated zest of 1 lemon
1 1/2 cups all-purpose flour
1/2 teaspoon baking powder
1/4 cup canned coconut cream
1 cup dried shredded coconut

1 Put an 8 x 1 1/2 inch round cake pan onto a sheet of waxed paper, trace around the bottom with a pencil and cut out a circle just inside the pencil marking. Brush the inside of the pan with melted butter and place the paper inside the pan. Preheat the oven to 350°F.

2 Prepare a caramel using the sugar and 3 tablespoons water, following the method in the Chef's techniques on page 62. After the caramel has stopped cooking, mix in the butter, then reheat the caramel and, when liquid, pour into the prepared cake pan. Set the pan aside for the caramel to cool. Carefully arrange the pineapple slices on top of the cooled caramel, trimming them to fit neatly into the cake pan if necessary, then decorate with the cherries.

3 To make the coconut sponge cake, put the butter and sugar in a bowl and, using a wooden spoon or electric mixer, beat until light and creamy. Add the eggs in six additions, beating well between each addition. Stir in the lemon zest, then sift the flour and baking powder into the mixture and beat in well with the coconut cream and dried shredded coconut until the mixture is smooth. Immediately spoon the coconut sponge cake on top of the pineapple slices and then make a slight hollow in the center of the mixture with the back of a damp spoon.

4 Bake for 1 hour, or until golden. To test when the cake is done, pierce with a skewer. If it comes out clean, the cake is cooked. Allow to stand for 5 minutes in the pan, then turn out and serve with cream or crème anglaise (see page 43).

Sussex pond pudding

Inside the light suet pastry is a combination of whole lemon, sugar and butter, which, when this unusually named pudding is cut, produces a "pond" of lemony sauce.

*Preparation time **30 minutes + 20 minutes standing***
*Total cooking time **3 hours***
*Serves **4–6***

FILLING
1 cup unsalted butter, softened
2/3 cup light brown sugar
2/3 cup Demerara or turbinado sugar
1 thin-skinned lemon, washed

CRUST
1 1/2 cups self-rising flour
grated zest of 1 lemon
1/3 cup grated suet (see page 63)
1/4 cup milk

1 Prepare a 4-cup pudding basin or heatproof glass bowl for steaming (see Chef's techniques, page 62).

2 To make the filling, put the butter and sugars in a bowl and, using a wooden spoon or electric mixer, beat together until soft and pale. Prick the lemon all over with a thick skewer.

3 To make the crust, sift together the flour and a pinch of salt into a bowl. Stir in the lemon zest and suet, then make a well in the center and pour the milk and 1/4 cup water into it. Using a palette knife, stir the flour into the liquid until combined into a soft dough. Lightly flour a clean surface, tip the dough onto it and knead for 5 seconds until smooth, then cut off and reserve one fourth for the top.

4 Roll out the remaining three-fourths of the dough to a circle large enough to fill the inside of the prepared basin or bowl. Transfer the dough to the basin or bowl and ease the pastry into the round bowl shape, without

wrinkling it, leaving a little pastry hanging over the sides.

5 Immediately place a third of the filling into the pastry-lined basin or bowl, then place the lemon centrally on top. Pack the remaining filling firmly around the lemon and fold the pastry edge over the filling. Roll out the remaining quarter of dough to the size of the top of the basin or bowl, dampen the edges and place on top of the filling to form a top. Press together the lining dough and top to seal well. Cover and steam for 3 hours, following the steaming method in the Chef's techniques on page 62.

6 Allow the pudding to stand for 20 minutes, then remove the string, foil and paper and turn out onto a deep serving dish to catch the sauce that will run out.

7 To serve, remove a portion of the crust and place on a serving plate with some of the filling. Carefully remove the lemon from the center of the pudding and cut into four or six portions. Serve a piece with each portion of the pudding and accompany with a lemon sorbet, ice cream or cream.

Chef's tips The suet crust will continue to soak up the filling as it stands and leaving it to stand will make it easier to cut.

It is important for the lightness of the dough that the crust be made and used as quickly as possible. This is so the bubbles formed by the liquid reacting with the self-raising flour are trapped in the pastry.

An orange or lime could also be used. If using the smaller lime, the pudding could be made in four individual pudding basins or bowls, with a lime placed in each.

For a variation, flavor the crust with ground cinnamon or ginger instead of grated lemon zest, or add golden raisins to the filling.

Iles flottantes

A traditional French dessert that means "floating islands," this is an irresistible combination of islands of soft almond meringue floating on a sea of crème anglaise.

*Preparation time **30 minutes + cooling***
*Total cooking time **55 minutes***
Serves 6

2/3 cup sliced almonds
1/3 cup sugar
fresh mint sprigs, to decorate

MERINGUES
4 egg whites
1/3–1/2 cup sugar

CREME ANGLAISE
2 cups milk
1 vanilla bean, split lengthwise
4 egg yolks
1/3 cup sugar

1 Preheat a broiler and toast the sliced almonds to golden brown, taking care not to burn them, then cool and crush lightly. Line a baking sheet with waxed paper.

2 Prepare a caramel using the sugar and 1/2 cup water and following the method in the Chef's techniques on page 62. After the caramel has stopped cooking, immediately stir in the almonds and pour this mixture onto the prepared baking sheet, being careful as the baking sheet will become very hot. Leave to cool.

3 Line the bottoms of six 1/2-cup pudding molds or ramekins with a disc of waxed paper. Using a palette knife or metal spatula, loosen the caramel-nut mixture and lift it off the baking sheet onto a board. With a heavy sharp knife, roughly chop into 1/2-inch pieces and scatter in the base of the molds. Preheat the oven to 275°F.

4 To make the meringues, beat the egg whites in a clean, dry bowl until soft peaks form. Add 1 tablespoon of the sugar and whisk well, then repeat until half the sugar has been added and the meringue is very stiff, smooth and satiny. Using a large metal spoon or plastic spatula, fold in the remaining half of the sugar.

5 Divide the mixture among the pudding molds or ramekins, tap them gently on the work surface to remove any air pockets, then level the tops with a palette knife. Cover each mold with a piece of lightly buttered, waxed paper and then place them in a baking pan or shallow dish. Pour boiling water around them to come halfway up the molds. Bake for about 15–20 minutes, or until a sharp knife inserted into the center of the meringue comes out clean.

6 To make the crème anglaise, pour the milk into a deep, heavy-bottomed saucepan over medium heat. Scrape the seeds from the vanilla bean and add to the milk along with the bean. Slowly bring just to a boil to allow the flavor of the vanilla to infuse into the milk. Remove from the heat. In a bowl, using a wooden spoon, cream together the yolks and the sugar until pale and thick. Pour the hot milk onto the yolks and mix well. Pour the mixture into a clean saucepan and cook over very gentle heat, stirring continuously, for about 5 minutes, or until it begins to thicken and coats the back of a spoon. Do not allow it to boil or it will curdle. Strain the sauce and discard the vanilla bean.

7 To serve, pour the crème anglaise onto six plates. Lift the molds out of the water bath and remove and discard the paper. If necessary, loosen the top edge of the meringues with a small knife, then unmold out onto the center of each plate and decorate with a mint sprig. Serve warm or cold.

Banana coconut fudge cake

*A sumptuously rich dessert where a layer of real vanilla fudge is topped with
sticky banana and coconut. Serve with a spoonful of crème fraîche.*

Preparation time **1 hour**
Total cooking time **1 hour 35 minutes**
Serves 6

FUDGE
2 vanilla beans
1 1/3 cups sugar
2/3 cup unsalted butter, cut into cubes
2/3 cup heavy cream

2/3 cup dried shredded coconut
4 bananas
3 eggs
1/2 teaspoon vanilla extract
1/2 cup sugar
1 cup all-purpose flour
1/2 teaspoon baking powder
3 tablespoons coconut cream
2 1/2 tablespoons milk
1 1/2 tablespoons unsalted butter, melted

1 Brush an 8-inch square or round cake pan (not one
with a removable bottom) with melted butter. Fold a
piece of waxed paper in half lengthwise and wrap
around the pan, folded-edge-downwards. Trim the paper
so it is 1 1/2 inches taller than the pan and the end is
3/4 inch longer than the circumference. Snip cuts along
the folded edge of the paper and place, cut-edge-down,
inside the pan. Cut two pieces of parchment paper to fit
the bottom of the pan, place in the pan and brush with
melted butter.
2 To make the fudge, prepare a caramel using the seeds
from the vanilla beans, the sugar and 1/2 cup water,
following the method in the Chef's techniques on page
62. After the caramel has stopped cooking, add the
butter and reheat, stirring gently to incorporate.
Remove from the heat, stir in the cream, then return the
pan to the stove and bring to a boil. Pour a fourth of the
fudge into the prepared pan and set aside to cool,
leaving the remaining fudge for later use. Sprinkle one
third of the coconut over the fudge in the pan.
3 Peel three of the bananas and cut them into 1/4-inch
thick slices. Mash the remaining banana and set aside.
Place the sliced bananas, slightly overlapping, on top of
the fudge and coconut in the pan. Preheat the oven to
warm 315°F.
4 Bring a saucepan half full of water to a boil, then
remove from the heat. Have ready a heatproof bowl
that will fit on top of the pan without actually touching
the water. Put the eggs, vanilla and sugar in the bowl and
place over the pan of steaming water. Whisk until the
mixture is thick and leaves a trail across the surface
when the whisk is lifted. Remove the bowl and continue
whisking until cold, then sift the flour and baking
powder onto the mixture and fold in gently using a large
metal spoon or plastic spatula.
5 In a large bowl, mix together the remaining coconut,
the mashed banana, coconut cream, milk and melted
butter, then fold gently into the mixture. Pour this cake
batter into the pan and bake for 1 hour 15 minutes. To
test when the cake is done, pierce with a skewer. If the
skewer comes out clean, the cake is cooked.
6 Turn out the cake immediately onto a serving plate.
Reheat the reserved fudge and serve the cake with the
fudge and some crème fraîche.

Tipsy cake

In Austria, where this cake originated, it is called "Besoffener Capuziner," which can be translated as Tipsy friar. In this version, there is enough rum for flavor, but not enough to make you tipsy!

Preparation time **45 minutes + 30 minutes soaking + 30 minutes infusing + 4 hours soaking**
Total cooking time **40 minutes**
Serves 6

PUDDING

1/2 cup raisins
2 tablespoons rum
4 eggs, separated
1/3 cup sugar
finely grated zest of 1 orange
1 cup white bread crumbs, sifted
1/3 cup ground almonds or almond meal
2 tablespoons milk
2 teaspoons unsweetened cocoa powder

SYRUP

1/2 cup water
1 cup sugar
1 vanilla bean
1 1/2 teaspoons coffee extract or 2 teaspoons instant coffee mixed with 1 teaspoon hot water
1 1/2 tablespoons rum
rind of 1 1/2 oranges
2 small cinnamon sticks
3 cloves

1 In a small bowl, soak the raisins in the rum for 30 minutes. Preheat the oven to 350°F. Brush a 4-cup, fluted ring mold, or tube or Bundt pan with melted butter, chill to set and brush again.

2 With an electric mixer, beat the egg yolks in a large bowl with half the sugar and the orange zest until pale and fluffy. Wash the beaters, dry thoroughly, and in another clean dry bowl, beat the egg whites until stiff. Add the remaining sugar in three batches, mixing well between each addition until stiff, glossy peaks form. Using a large metal spoon or plastic spatula, fold one third of the meringue into the yolk mixture, followed by half each of the bread crumbs, almonds and milk. Repeat, then fold in the remaining meringue. Remove one third of the mixture to a separate bowl, sift the cocoa powder into this smaller amount of cake mixture and fold in gently.

3 Drain the raisins, reserving any rum. Place half the raisins in the bottom of the pan and sprinkle the remainder onto the white cake mixture and barely fold in with two or three strokes of the spoon. Place alternate spoonfuls of the white and chocolate cake mixtures into the pan, swirling once or twice with the handle of a spoon or spatula to get a good marbled effect. Finish with the white mixture. Bake for 30–35 minutes, or until the cake is golden brown and a skewer inserted into the center comes out clean.

4 To make the syrup, place all the ingredients in a saucepan with any reserved rum from the raisins and slowly bring to a boil, then remove from the stove and leave to stand and infuse for 30 minutes.

5 Loosen the edge of the cake with a palette knife and turn out onto a plate or wire rack. Replace the pan and turn over again so the cake is loose but in the pan. Strain two thirds of the syrup over the cake, allow it to cool, then cover with plastic wrap and leave at cool room temperature for 4 hours.

6 Turn out the cake and serve with the remaining syrup. Fill the center of the cake with sweetened whipped cream or just serve some whipped cream on the side.

Chef's tip For a variation, use Tia Maria instead of rum.

Chocolate soufflé with crème de menthe sauce

A delicious chocolate soufflé accompanied by a light sauce of eggs, sugar and crème de menthe, which is known as "zabaglione" to the Italians and "sabayon" to the French.

Preparation time **25 minutes + 10 minutes cooling**
Total cooking time **1 hour**
Serves 4–6

2 oz. good-quality dark chocolate, preferably bitter, roughly chopped
1/2 cup milk
2 tablespoons unsweetened cocoa powder
2 tablespoons all-purpose flour, sifted
2 tablespoons sugar
1/4 teaspoon vanilla extract
3 egg yolks
4 egg whites
unsweetened cocoa powder, to dust
chocolate curls, to decorate, optional

SAUCE
1 egg
3 egg yolks
2 1/2 tablespoons sugar
1 1/2 tablespoons white crème de menthe

1 Brush a 6-cup charlotte mold with some melted butter, dust it with sugar, then lightly tap and empty out any excess sugar. Half fill a saucepan that will sit beneath a vegetable or bamboo steamer with water and slowly bring to a boil.

2 Place the chocolate in a bowl and pour the milk into a small saucepan. Bring the milk to a boil, then pour onto the chocolate and stir with a wooden spoon until the chocolate is melted and the mixture smooth. Return the mixture to the pan with the cocoa and bring just to a boil. Add the flour and quickly beat together with a wooden spoon over low heat for 2 minutes, or until the mixture is smooth and rolls away readily from the bottom and side of the pan. Remove from the stove, stir in the sugar and vanilla and cool for about 10 minutes, or until lukewarm. Add the yolks one at a time, beating the mixture well between each addition.

3 Put the egg whites into a clean dry bowl and whisk with a hand whisk or electric mixer until stiff peaks form. Using a large metal spoon or plastic spatula, quickly fold 1 tablespoon of egg white into the chocolate mixture to soften it, then carefully fold in the remaining egg white.

4 Immediately pour the mixture into the prepared mold and cover with plastic wrap. Place it in the basket over the boiling water. Turn the heat down to a gentle simmer, cover the steamer with a lid "almost on" or a piece of aluminum foil pierced with a few holes. Steam with the water gently bubbling for about 40–45 minutes, or until well risen and firm to the touch. Remove the mold from the steamer and set aside while making the sauce.

5 To make the sauce, place all the ingredients in a heatproof bowl that can sit over the water in the saucepan. Lightly whisk the ingredients together, then place the bowl over the steaming water and continue to whisk until the mixture is light and frothy and when the whisk is lifted just above the surface, the sauce falls back to leave a ribbon-like trail.

6 To serve, remove the plastic wrap from the soufflé and turn out onto a plate. Dust with the cocoa and decorate with chocolate curls. Serve immediately with the sauce.

Chef's tips The soufflé will turn out easily if left to stand for 5 minutes. Do not leave it in the steamer or it will overcook in its own residual heat.

Do not make the sauce in advance because it may separate and become liquid at the bottom if left to stand.

Eton mess

Named after the famous English school, this easy-to-make dessert is perfect for summer's abundance of strawberries. A great way to use up overripe fruit and leftover or broken meringues.

Preparation time **25 minutes + 4 hours marinating**
Total cooking time **None**
Serves 4

1 1/4 lb. strawberries, hulled
4 tablespoons Grand Marnier
1 vanilla bean, split lengthwise
3 tablespoons sugar
2 store-bought meringues
1 2/3 cups heavy cream, for whipping .

1 Set aside four good strawberries for decoration. Put the remaining strawberries in a large bowl and roughly crush with a fork. Add the Grand Marnier, vanilla bean and sugar, cover with plastic wrap and marinate in the refrigerator for at least 4 hours. Remove and discard the vanilla bean, then spoon one third of the mixture into four wine glasses. Break the meringues roughly into about 1/2-inch pieces.

2 Pour the cream into a bowl and, using a hand whisk or electric mixer, whip the cream until just thick, but so that it still runs if the bowl is tipped.

3 Add the cream to the remaining two thirds of the strawberry mixture and, using a large metal spoon or plastic spatula, fold together until streaky and half combined. Add two thirds of the broken meringues and continue to fold until evenly combined.

4 Spoon the meringue mixture onto the crushed strawberries in the wine glasses. Crush the remaining meringues a little more and sprinkle over the surface, then decorate with a whole strawberry. Serve immediately while the meringue is still crunchy.

Plum charlotte

Usually made with apple, this plum charlotte is a delicious variation on a classic. Careful lining of the mold will ensure that the charlotte turns out beautifully.

Preparation time **35 minutes + 1 hour cooling**
Total cooking time **55 minutes**
Serves 6

17 thin slices of white bread, trimmed of crusts
2 cups unsalted butter
1 cup white bread crumbs
1/2 cup light brown sugar
2 lb. red plums, fresh or canned, pitted and
   cut into 1/2-inch pieces
a little lemon rind
pinch of ground cinnamon
1/4 cup apricot jam

1 Brush an 8-cup charlotte mold or soufflé dish with a little melted butter. Cut six slices of bread in half to form rectangles and cut seven slices in half at a diagonal to form triangles. Reserve the remaining four slices.
2 Turn the mold upside down and place the bread triangles on top, overlapping the edges to completely cover the top of the mold. Hold the triangles in place and, using the mold as a guide, trim the excess edges with scissors so the triangles will fit inside the base of the mold exactly. Reserve the trimmings.
3 Melt 1 1/2 cups of the butter in a pan, dip the bread triangles in, then line the base of the mold, butter-side-down. Dip the rectangles in butter and arrange around the sides, butter-side-out, overlapping the edges until the mold is completely covered and filling any gaps with the bread trimmings. Dip the reserved slices of bread in the butter and set aside.

4 To make the filling, melt half the remaining butter in a large pan, add the bread crumbs and cook, stirring, until golden brown. Drain on crumpled paper towels. In another pan, gently heat the remaining butter and the brown sugar, stir well to dissolve, then cook without stirring until light caramel in color. Add the plums and gently cook, stirring frequently, until just starting to soften (if you are using canned plums, you will only need to heat them through). Remove from the stove, add the lemon rind, cinnamon and bread crumbs and stir gently to combine.
5 Preheat the oven to 375°F. Ladle the filling into the prepared mold until half full. Cover with half the reserved bread slices, press down firmly to level, then add the remaining filling. If the filling is not level with the mold lining, trim the bread with a small knife or scissors. Cover with the remaining bread pieces, butter-side-up, taking care to fill any gaps. Press in gently and cover with aluminum foil.
6 Place the charlotte on a baking sheet and bake for about 40 minutes, or until golden and firm. Leave for about 1 hour to cool completely before turning out onto a serving plate.
7 In a small pan, heat the apricot jam with about 1 1/2 tablespoons water. When the mixture has melted and begins to boil, strain it into a small bowl and, while still hot, brush it over the surface of the charlotte.

Chef's tip Some varieties of plums have thicker skins than others. If you wish to remove the skins, dip the plums in boiling water for 10–20 seconds, quickly cool in ice water, then skin before removing pits.

Steamed orange pudding

*Hot, light and full of flavor, this steamed pudding will brighten the gloom of a winter's day like
a burst of summer sunshine. Serve with the orange sauce or custard sauce.*

Preparation time **30 minutes**
Total cooking time **1 hour 45 minutes**
Serves 6

1/3 cup thin-cut marmalade
2 large oranges, peel and pith removed
1/2 cup unsalted butter, at room temperature
1/2 cup sugar
finely grated rind of 1 orange
2 large eggs, beaten
1 1/2 cups self-rising flour
milk, for mixing

SAUCE
3/4 cup orange juice
2 egg yolks
1/2 teaspoon cornstarch
3 tablespoons sugar
1 teaspoon Grand Marnier or Cointreau

1 Prepare a 5-cup pudding basin or heatproof glass
bowl for steaming (see Chef's techniques, page 62).
2 Spoon the marmalade into the basin or bowl. Finely
slice the oranges, then line the basin or bowl with the
slices, from the marmalade base to the top of the basin.
3 In a bowl, beat the butter with a wooden spoon or
electric mixer to soften. Slowly add the sugar, beating
until light and creamy. Mix in the orange rind. Add the
egg in six additions, beating well between each addition.
Sift in the flour and quickly fold into the mixture using
a large metal spoon or plastic spatula. As the last traces
of flour are mixed in, add a little milk to form a soft
consistency: the mixture should drop from the spoon
with a flick of the wrist.

4 Immediately spoon the mixture into the prepared
basin or bowl, cover and steam for 1 1/2–1 3/4 hours,
following the steaming method in the Chef's techniques
on page 62. To test if the pudding is done, pierce with a
skewer. If it comes out clean, the pudding is cooked.

5 Remove the string, foil and paper and turn the
pudding out onto a serving plate (if you are not serving
the pudding immediately, place the bowl back over the
pudding to prevent it from drying out).

6 To make the sauce, bring the orange juice to a boil in
a small saucepan. In a bowl, beat the egg yolks,
cornstarch and sugar until thick and light. Pour the hot
orange juice into the bowl, mix until blended, then
return to the pan. Cook over medium heat, stirring
constantly with a wooden spoon, until the mixture coats
the back of the spoon and the sauce does not close over
when a line is drawn across the spoon with a finger.

7 Remove from the heat, strain into a bowl, then stir in
the Grand Marnier or Cointreau. If you are not using
the sauce straight away, dust the surface lightly with
sugar to prevent a skin from forming. The sugar can be
stirred in just before serving. Serve the sauce warm or
cold with the pudding.

Lemon delicious

Also known as "Lemon surprise," this wonderful dessert separates as it cooks
into a light soufflé sponge topping with a tart lemon sauce hidden beneath.

*Preparation time **25 minutes***
*Total cooking time **40 minutes***
Serves 4

1/4 cup unsalted butter, at room temperature
1/3 cup sugar
finely grated zest of I lemon
2 large eggs, separated
2 tablespoons all-purpose flour
3 tablespoons lemon juice
I cup milk
confectioner's sugar, for dusting

1 Preheat the oven to 350°F. Brush with melted butter an 81/4 x 6 x 13/4 inch ovenproof dish. .

2 Using a wooden spoon or electric mixer, beat the butter to soften it, then beat in the sugar in small additions. Continue beating until the mixture is light and creamy, then mix in the lemon zest and egg yolks until well blended. Gently fold in the flour, followed by the lemon juice.

3 In a small saucepan, warm the milk until tepid, then fold it into the lemon mixture.

4 Put the egg whites in a large clean dry bowl, add a pinch of salt and beat them with a hand whisk or electric mixer until soft peaks form. Using a plastic spatula or a large metal spoon, mix 1 tablespoon of the egg white into the lemon mixture to soften it, then carefully fold in the remaining egg white, being careful not to lose volume.

5 Pour the mixture into the prepared dish, then set in a baking pan or shallow ovenproof dish and pour warm water around to come about two thirds up the sides. Bake for 30–35 minutes, or until the top is a pale golden brown and firm to the light touch of a finger. Serve the pudding hot or chilled. If you are serving cold, dust with a little sifted confectioner's sugar.

Chef's tip When the lemon juice meets the butter, the mixture may curdle. However, when you add the milk, the mixture should become smooth again (make sure the milk is barely warm—if it is too hot, the flour and yolks may cook and the mixture become too heavy).

Traditional rice pudding

This classic favorite, so simple to prepare, cooks slowly and gently in the oven, allowing the rice time to absorb all the liquid. The result is delightfully soft and creamy.

*Preparation time **5 minutes + 30 minutes resting***
*Total cooking time **2 hours***
Serves 4

3 cups milk
1 1/2 tablespoons sugar
2–3 drops vanilla extract
1/3 cup short-grain rice
unsalted butter, for topping
freshly grated nutmeg, to taste

1 Combine the milk, sugar, vanilla extract and rice in a 4-cup pie plate or ovenproof dish and leave to rest for 30 minutes. Preheat the oven to 350°F.
2 Dot the butter over the mixture, sprinkle some nutmeg over the top and cover with aluminum foil.

Place the dish on the middle shelf of the oven and bake for 1 hour, stirring once or twice with a fork.
3 Remove the foil and reduce the oven temperature to 300°F. If serving the pudding cold, bake for another 45 minutes, leave to cool, then refrigerate until ready to serve. If serving hot, cook for 1 hour, or until a brown skin forms and the interior of the pudding is soft and creamy. Serve hot with a teaspoon of strawberry jam or cold with poached red plums.

Chef's tips If the rice pudding is too dry, adjust the consistency before serving by lifting the skin to one side and adding a little cold milk.

To vary the flavor of this pudding, use cinnamon in place of the vanilla and the nutmeg, or sprinkle some golden raisins or chopped candied citrus in with the rice before cooking.

Chocolate fondant soufflés

The "fondant" aspect of these simple but marvelously effective chocolate fixes is the hot center,
which spills slowly across the plate when the crisp shell of the soufflé is broken open.

*Preparation time **35 minutes + 5 minutes cooling***
*Total cooking time **20 minutes***
Serves 6

4 oz. bittersweet chocolate, chopped
1/2 cup unsalted butter, at room temperature
2 eggs
2 egg yolks
1/3 cup sugar
2 teaspoons unsweetened cocoa powder
1/2 cup bread flour
3/4 teaspoon baking powder
unsweetened cocoa powder, for dusting

1 Thickly brush six 1/2-cup ramekins with some melted butter, dust with sugar, then lightly tap and empty out any excess sugar. Preheat the oven to 350°F.
2 Bring a saucepan half full of water to a boil, then remove from the heat. Have ready a heatproof bowl that will fit over the pan without actually touching the water. Put the chocolate and butter in the bowl and place over the pan of steaming water. Leave to stand until the chocolate has melted, then stir with a wooden spoon until the butter is incorporated and the mixture is smooth and glossy. Remove the bowl from over the saucepan and allow to cool for 5 minutes.
3 Put the whole eggs, yolks and sugar in another bowl and whisk until pale and thick. Fold into the chocolate mixture using a large metal spoon (the mixture should not be totally incorporated at this stage).
4 Sift the cocoa powder, flour and baking powder onto the mixture and, using a large metal spoon or plastic spatula, fold in gently until no pale streaks are visible. Pour the mixture into the prepared ramekins and bake for 15–18 minutes.
5 When the puddings are cooked, allow them to stand for 2 minutes, then turn out and dust with cocoa powder. Serve immediately with raspberries and whipped cream.

Chef's tip The molten center of these soufflés is dependent on a very precise cooking time. Since all ovens vary slightly in temperature, if you are making these for a special occasion, you may wish to do a practice run first.

Chef's techniques

◆

Steaming puddings

Make sure your pudding basin or heatproof glass bowl will fit in your pan with the lid on.

Thickly brush a pudding basin or heatproof glass bowl with melted butter. Line the base of the basin or bowl with a disk of waxed paper.

Lay a sheet of aluminum foil on the work surface and cover with a sheet of waxed paper. Make a large pleat in the middle and brush the paper with some melted butter.

Place the mixture in the basin or bowl and hollow the surface slightly with the back of a wet spoon. Place the foil, paper-side-down, across the top and tie string around the rim and over the top to make a handle.

Place a saucer or trivet in a large pan and rest the basin or bowl on it. Half-fill the pan with boiling water and bring to a boil. Cover and simmer until cooked, adding more boiling water if needed.

Making caramel

Using water to dissolve your sugar gives a greater degree of control for caramel-making.

Place the granulated sugar and water in a heavy-bottomed saucepan. Fill a shallow pan with cold water and set it next to the stove.

Stir over low heat to dissolve the sugar. To prevent sugar crystals from forming, brush down the sides of the pan with a brush dipped in water.

Bring to a boil and simmer until the caramel takes on a deep golden color. Swirl the pan to stop the caramel from coloring unevenly.

Stop the cooking by plunging the bottom of the pan into the cold water for a few seconds.

Making crêpes

A crêpe pan makes crêpe-making much easier, especially if you keep it just for this.

Over medium heat, melt some clarified butter or oil in a 6–7 inch heavy-bottomed or non-stick saucepan. When a haze forms, pour out any excess butter.

Stir the batter well and pour into the pan from a ladle, starting in the center and swirling the pan to create a thin coating. Tip out any excess.

Cook for 1 minute until bubbles appear, the batter sets and the edges are brown. Carefully loosen and lift the edges with a palette knife. Turn and cook for 30 seconds until golden. Remove from the pan and repeat.

Grating suet

If ready-prepared suet is not available, make your own by grating fresh suet.

Prepare the suet by grating it by hand or by using a food processor.

Making baba dough

Using your hand to mix baba dough is more effective than a spoon.

Using the fingers of one hand, held lightly apart, bring the ingredients together to form a soft elastic dough. Mix with the hand for about 5 minutes, or until smooth.

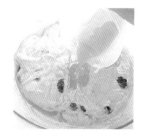

Add the raisins and rum and mix with your hand to combine. Scrape down the sides of the bowl and pour the warm butter over the surface of the dough.

Cover and leave to rise for about 30 minutes, or until doubled in volume. Mix the baba mixture to incorporate the butter.

Spoon the mixture into a pastry bag fitted with a 3/4-inch plain tip and pipe into the molds. Cover with a damp cloth and prove until the mixture reaches the tops of the molds.

First published in the United States in 2000 by Periplus Editions (HK) Ltd., with editorial offices at
153 Milk Street, Boston, Massachusetts 02109.

Murdoch Books and Le Cordon Bleu thank the 32 masterchefs of all the Le Cordon Bleu Schools, whose knowledge and
expertise have made this book possible, especially: Chef Terrien, Chef Boucheret, Chef Duchêne (MOF), Chef Guillut,
Chef Pinaud, Paris; Chef Males, Chef Walsh, Chef Power, Chef Neveu, Chef Paton, Chef Poole-Gleed, Chef Wavrin, London;
Chef Chantefort, Chef Nicaud, Chef Jambert, Chef Honda, Tokyo; Chef Salambien, Chef Boutin, Chef Harris, Sydney;
Chef Lawes, Adelaide; Chef Guiet, Chef Denis, Chef Petibon, Chef Jean Michel Poncet, Ottawa.
Of the many students who helped the Chefs test each recipe, a special mention to graduates Hollace Hamilton and Alice Buckley.
A very special acknowledgment to Helen Barnard, Alison Oakervee and Deepika Sukhwani, who have been responsible for the
coordination of the Le Cordon Bleu team throughout this series under the Presidency of André Cointreau.

First published in Australia in 1999 by Murdoch Books®

Series Manager: Kay Halsey
Series Concept, Design and Art Direction: Juliet Cohen
Food Editor: Lulu Grimes
Designer: Norman Baptista
Photographers: Jon Bader, Craig Cranko
Food Stylists: Kay Francis, Mary Harris
Food Preparation: Michelle Earl, Kerrie Mullins
Chef's Techniques Photographer: Reg Morrison
Home Economists: Michelle Earl, Michelle Lawton, Michaela Le Compte, Maria Villegas

Library of Congress catalog card number: 99-068926
ISBN 962-593-822-2

Front cover: Summer puddings

Distributed in the United States by
Tuttle Publishing
Distribution Center
Airport Industrial Park
364 Innovation Drive
North Clarendon, VT 05759-9436
Tel: (802) 773-8930
Tel: (800) 526-2778

PRINTED IN SINGAPORE

06 05 04 03 02 01 00 10 9 8 7 6 5 4 3 2 1

Important: Some of the recipes in this book may include raw eggs, which can cause salmonella poisoning.
Those who might be at risk from this (the elderly, pregnant women, young children and those suffering
from immune deficiency diseases) should check with their physicians before eating raw eggs.